I0116889

Take Action®

Child Handout Workbook

Contents

Who can use Take Action?

The evidence-base for Take Action has been established with the program being delivered by registered psychologists, clinical psychologists, school psychologists and school guidance counsellors who are trained and experienced in Cognitive-Behavioural Therapy (CBT). Therefore, Take Action is recommended for use by these mental health and educational professionals. This Child Handout Workbook should only be used in conjunction with the Take Action Practitioner Guidebook

www.
AUSTRALIANACADEMIC**PRESS**
.com.au

Other titles in the Take Action program:

Take Action Parent Handout Workbook

Take Action Practitioner Guidebook

Take Action Child Handout Workbook
First published 2016
Australian Academic Press Group Pty. Ltd.
18 Victor Russell Drive
Samford Valley QLD 4520
Australia
www.australianacademicpress.com.au

ISBN 9781922117281

Publisher: Stephen May

Cover and text design: Maria Biaggini of The Letter Tree

Cartoons and illustrations: Karen Mounsey-Smith of Gidgeymo Illustrations

Typesetting: Australian Academic Press

Printing; Lightning Source

Take Action

The Interview Exercise

We are going to get to know each other, as well as learn about how the Take Action program can help you. Your first activity is to find out the answers to the questions below.

Ask your new friend sitting beside you the following questions and write down their answers.

1. What is your friend's full name?

   _____

2. What is your friend's favourite TV show?

   _____

3. What is your friend's favourite book to read?

   _____

4. What is your friend's favourite computer game?

   _____

5. What grade is your friend in at school?

   _____

6. How many brothers and sisters does your friend have?

   _____

Congratulations! You have completed your first activity in the Take Action program!

A Step One

I can be AWARE of my Anxious Feelings and Body Signals.

WELCOME to the Take Action program!

You will learn how to take ACTION against your fears and worries so that you can enjoy things more and be happier!

Dulcy and Dion, your two new dolphin friends, will be learning to take ACTION with you.

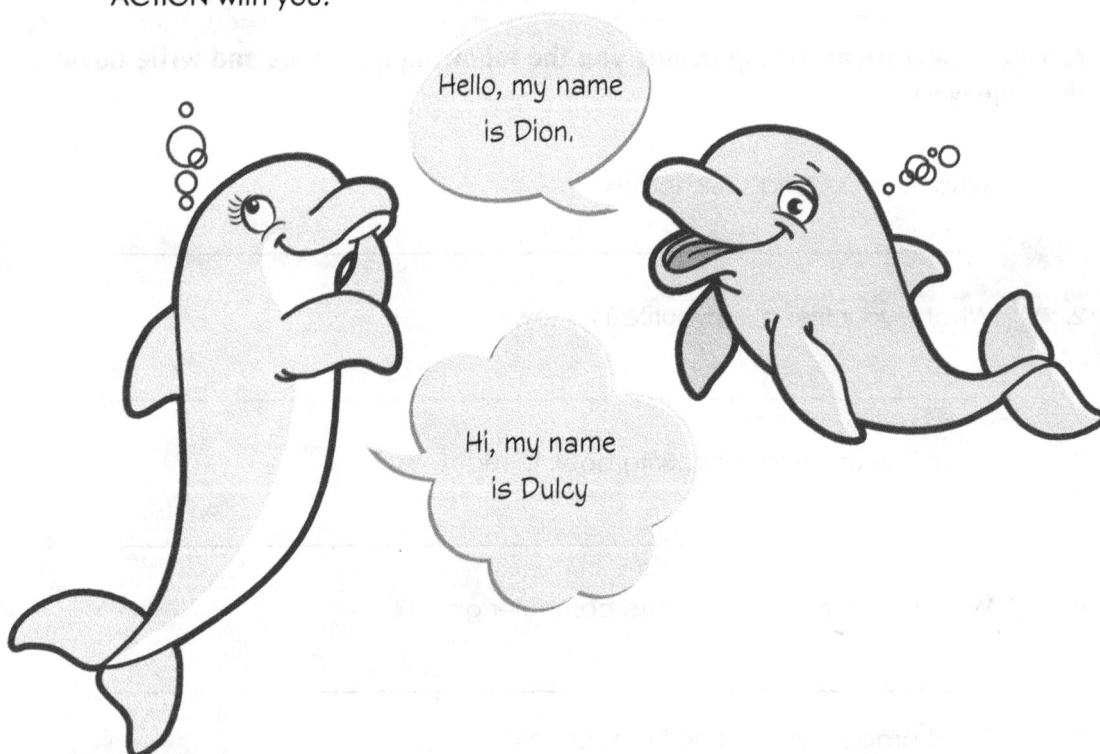

Hello, my name is Dion.

Hi, my name is Dulcy

Dulcy and Dion both think that it is normal to feel scared or worried when you are in danger. Everyone feels scared or worried at some time — it is a normal part of life.

Sometimes we get scared when there is NO real danger.

Situations like being in the dark, or being away from Mum or Dad, or making new friends might seem scary but they are not dangerous.

You can learn to feel better about anything that scares or worries you by taking ACTION.

Dion knows that children and adults get scared or worried sometimes for different reasons, but he has a question for you:

Activity
What is Anxiety?

Write down all the words you can think of that are used to describe anxiety on the lines below:

____

____

____

____

____

____

____

____

Now you know what anxiety means, it is time to learn about your ACTION Plan.

You will learn the six steps in the ACTION plan during the Take Action program. Each step will help you to take action against anxiety. By the end of the program, you will have an ACTION plan to keep and use in the future.

A C T I O N

Step One:
I can be **AWARE** of my Anxious Feelings and Body Signals.

Step Two:
I can keep **CALM** by doing On the Spot Deep Breathing and Move my Muscles Relaxation.

Step Three:
I can **THINK** Strong Thoughts.

Step Four:
I can get **INTO** Action by climbing the steps of my Action Ladder and rewarding myself.

Step Five:
I can use my **OPTIONS** including Problem Solving, Strong Team, and to Focus on the Positives. I can use my social skills to be more Strong, Confident and Assertive, and Deal with Bullies.

Step Six:
I will **NEVER** stop taking action against anxiety.

You are learning to take action against anxiety so you can enjoy things more and be happy!

Now we have worked out how to take ACTION together, Dulcy and Dion would like to tell you a story about themselves.

Dulcy and Dion the dolphins are really good friends. Dulcy and Dion are scared about learning to swim but they don't want to miss out on all the fun.

Dulcy is scared of the swimming teacher Mrs Seahorse because she has a loud voice. Dulcy is afraid Mrs Seahorse will think she is a bad swimmer and yell at her.

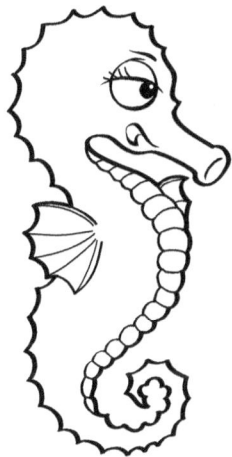

HURRY UP NOW!!

Dion is scared of swimming in the deep end.

But Dulcy says to herself: "Mrs Seahorse has a loud voice but she knows I am a beginner. I will try my best and the swimming lesson will be fun."

Dion says to himself: "I have swum in the deep end before on holidays and nothing bad happened to me. I can do it again."

Dulcy and Dion were scared about learning to swim at first, but they took ACTION against their fears by thinking Strong thoughts. They found out that they could have fun at their swimming lesson.

Activity
My Take ACTION Goals

Read the Worry Wall below and think about when you feel anxious.

Being away from mum or dad or home	Of certain things e.g. darkness, animals	In situations with other people e.g. doing a speech
School e.g. grades, homework, assignments	Performance e.g. being good in things like sports	Social e.g. making friends, what others think of you
Little things e.g. what happened in the past	Perfectionism e.g. never making mistakes	Health of yourself or others
Family e.g. money worries	Things going on in the world e.g. war, natural disasters	Other worries

Write down when you feel anxious on the lines below.

I feel extremely anxious when:

_____

I feel a lot of anxiety when:

_____

I feel a little bit of anxiety when:

_____

I feel calm and relaxed when:

_____

From the lists above, think about the worries or fears that you would like to take ACTION against. Write your Take ACTION goals on the lines below:

_____

_____

Be AWARE of Anxious Feelings

A great way to work out how you are feeling in different situations is the **Feelometer**.

The **Feelometer** is just like a thermometer that can tell your temperature.

You can use the **Feelometer** to know how anxious you are feeling at different times.

Look at the **Feelometer** below:

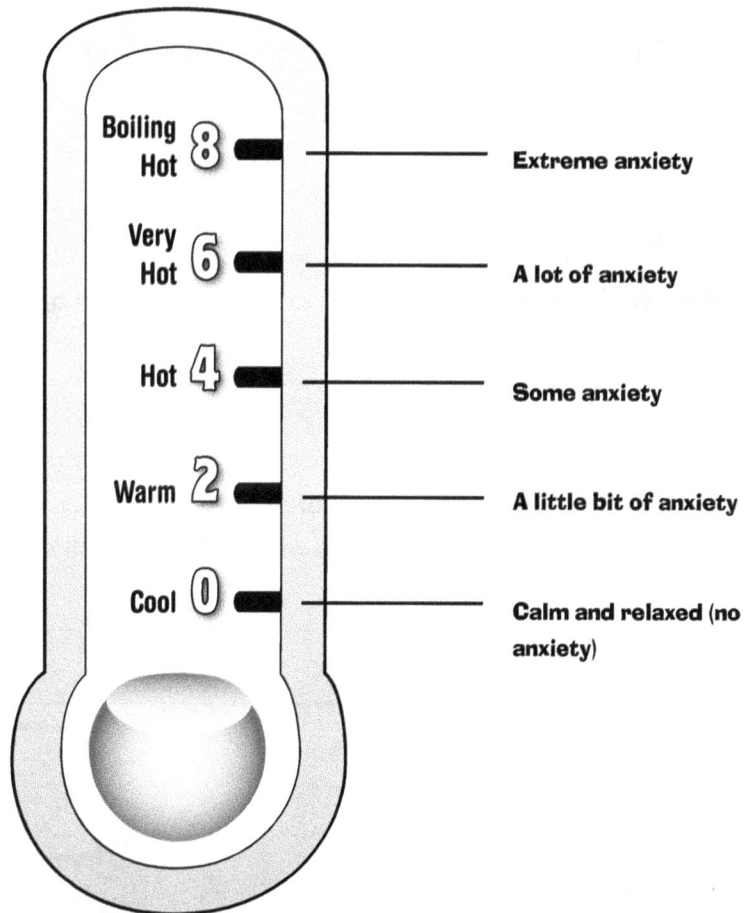

Boiling Hot	8	**Extreme anxiety**
Very Hot	6	**A lot of anxiety**
Hot	4	**Some anxiety**
Warm	2	**A little bit of anxiety**
Cool	0	**Calm and relaxed (no anxiety)**

Activity
Using the Feelometer

If you rated your anxiety levels as **cool** on the Feelometer, you would feel calm and relaxed (no anxiety at all). Write down a time when you have felt **calm and relaxed**:

_____

_____

If you rated your anxiety levels as **warm** on the Feelometer, you would be feeling a little bit of anxiety. Write down a time when you have felt **a little bit of anxiety**:

_____

_____

If you rated your anxiety levels as **hot** on the Feelometer, you would be feeling some anxiety. Write down a time when you have felt **some anxiety**:

_____

_____

If you rated your anxiety levels as **very hot** on the Feelometer, you would be feeling a lot of anxiety. Write down a time when you have felt **a lot of anxiety**:

_____

_____

If you rated your anxiety levels as **boiling hot** on the Feelometer, you would be feeling extreme anxiety. Write down a time when you have felt **extreme anxiety**:

_____

_____

You can use the Feelometer to tell you how anxious you are feeling. To be AWARE of your anxious feelings and the times when you need to Take ACTION is part of the first step in the ACTION plan.

Be AWARE: Anxiety is a Good Alarm and a False Alarm

Anxiety is a common emotion that we all experience. Everyone feels scared or worried at some time — it is a normal part of life. Anxiety is a signal that there is danger. In the caveman days, it was very important for cavemen to get scared if they saw a sabre-tooth tiger so they could either fight the tiger or run away to safety.

> That's a tiger. He could eat me! Should I run or fight?

Real DANGER!

As soon as the caveman saw the sabre-tooth tiger, the caveman's brain would send messages of danger to his body, making his heart beat fast and his hands cold. He might also sweat a lot and get butterflies in his stomach. These changes in his body would help him to take ACTION and survive because he could either fight the tiger if he had to, or run away from the tiger to safety.

Children and adults get the same changes in their bodies today. If we have to fight or escape from a dangerous situation, our bodies change to help us to be strong and take ACTION. This is when anxiety is helpful! It is normal to feel scared when you are in real danger — just like the caveman.
Sometimes we have 'false alarms' and we feel scared in our bodies when there is no real danger. When there is a 'false alarm', we feel **Boiling Hot** on the Feelometer when we should feel **Cool** (this is happening to the boy below). You can be AWARE of these 'false alarms', by working out how anxious you feel on the Feelometer.

> What if my friends don't talk to me tomorrow?

False ALARM

> Anxiety is only helpful when there is real danger. Be AWARE of 'false alarms'.

Be AWARE of Anxious Body Signals

Dulcy has listened to her body and she has noticed these Anxious Body Signals (see them below). The hotter Dulcy feels on the Feelometer, the more Anxious Body Signals she has.

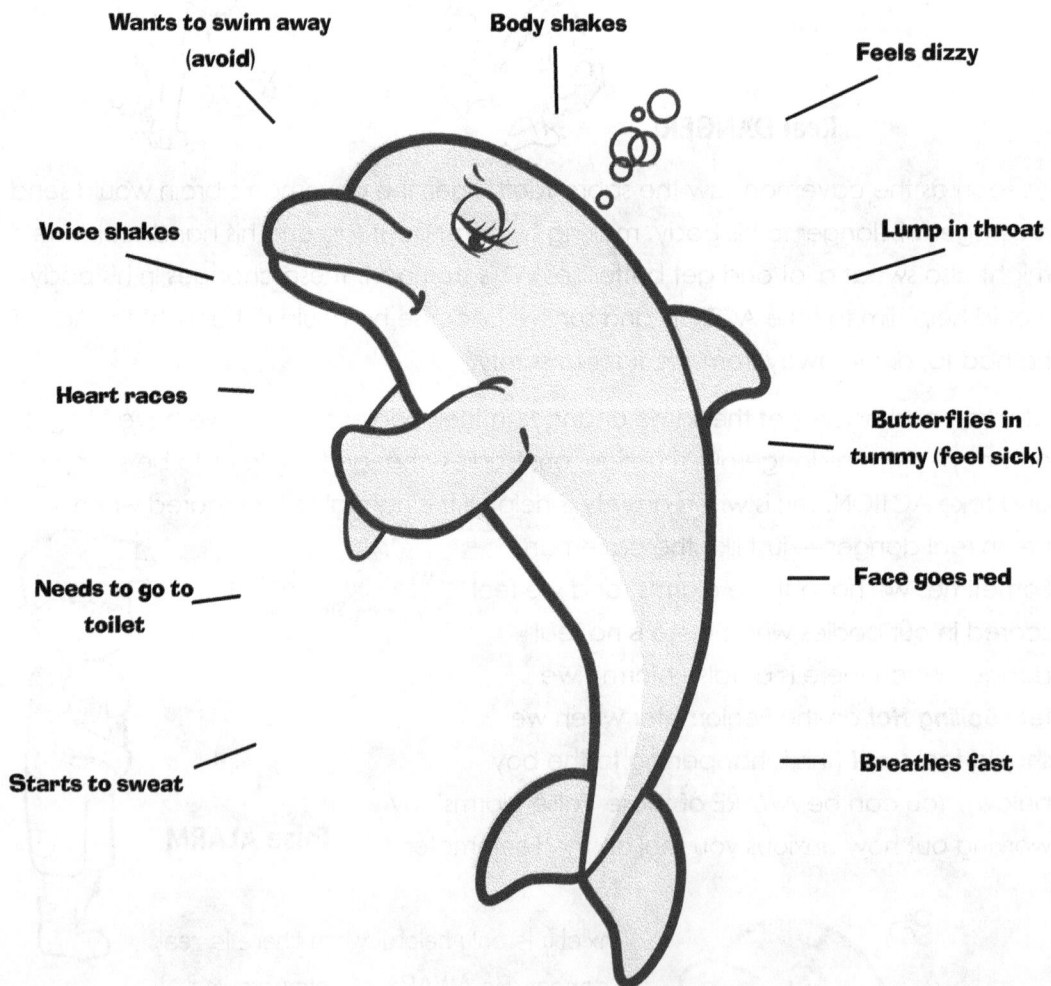

Wants to swim away (avoid)

Body shakes

Feels dizzy

Voice shakes

Lump in throat

Heart races

Butterflies in tummy (feel sick)

Needs to go to toilet

Face goes red

Starts to sweat

Breathes fast

Take Action

Activity
Be AWARE of Your
Anxious Body Signals

Work out which Anxious Body Signals you get when you feel anxious.

Think of a time when you felt anxious and write it down:

_____

Rate your Feelings on the Feelometer: _____

Colour in the Anxious Body Signals shown below that you had when you felt anxious.

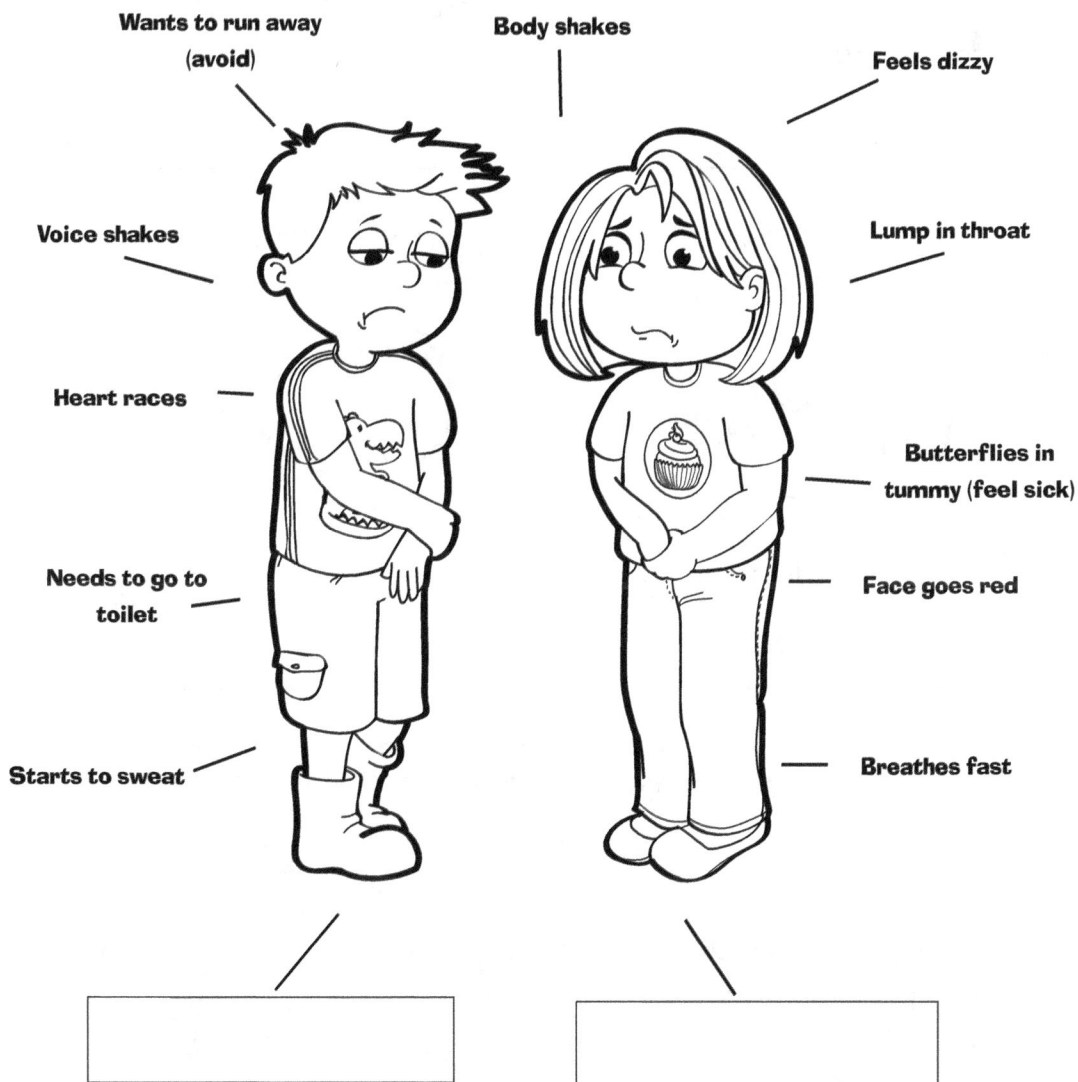

Wants to run away (avoid)

Body shakes

Feels dizzy

Voice shakes

Lump in throat

Heart races

Butterflies in tummy (feel sick)

Needs to go to toilet

Face goes red

Starts to sweat

Breathes fast

Add in any other Anxious Body Signals that are not listed.

Activity
Be AWARE of Feelings on Faces

Another way you can be AWARE of false alarms is by the look on other people's faces. If you feel anxious but other people look calm or happy, it could be a false alarm. Look at the faces below and write down the correct feeling for each one.

What feeling/s is this face showing?

_____

What feeling/s is this face showing?

_____

What feeling/s is this face showing?

_____

What feeling/s is this face showing?

_____

Knowing how you are feeling helps you go from Hot to Cool on the Feelometer, and 'stops false alarms'.

Whenever you feel anxious, Stop, Look at other people's faces for clues about how to feel, and Learn from your Anxious Body Signals so you can take ACTION.

Be AWARE of Different Feelings

Just like there are lots of different sea animals living in the ocean, there are lots of different feelings that we can feel.

This is Dulcy the dolphin

Dulcy likes to dive in and out of the water. Dulcy feels HAPPY. She feels so happy when she swims in and out of the water with her friends. Sometimes we feel happy like Dulcy the dolphin.

This is Claire the clam

Claire stays inside her shell. She feels SCARED. She does not want to leave her shell in case she gets eaten. Sometimes we feel scared like Claire the clam.

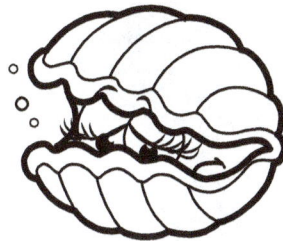

This is Wendy the whale

Wendy swims through the sea all on her own. Wendy feels SAD. She sings a sad whale song that you can hear under the sea. Sometimes we feel sad like Wendy the whale.

This is Shawn the shark

Shawn does not like it when he gets caught in a shark net. Shawn feels ANGRY. He yells and hits the shark net with his fins. Sometimes we feel angry like Shawn the shark.

This is Tommy the turtle

Tommy surfs the current in the sea. Tommy feels CALM. Tommy feels so cool when he surfs with his friends. Sometimes we feel calm like Tommy the turtle.

Dulcy feels HAPPY

Wendy feels SAD

Tommy feels CALM

Shawn feels ANGRY

Claire feels SCARED

Take Action

Activity
Be AWARE of Your Feelings

Read the story about Olivia and answer the questions below.

Olivia was having lots of fun playing outside in her backyard. She had been out there nearly all day. Then, her mum said that she was going to the shops and she would be back in 20 minutes. Olivia does not like her mum going anywhere without her.

How do you think Olivia felt when her mum said she was going to the shops?

_____

Circle the face which matches Olivia's feeling:

Write down a time when you have felt like Olivia:

_____

Rate your Feelings on the Feelometer:

_____

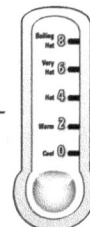

What did you say or do when you felt like Olivia?

_____

Did you do anything to help yourself feel better during this time?

_____

_____

Take Action

Activity
Be AWARE of Your Feelings

Read the story about Paul and answer the questions below.

Paul just got an ice-cream from the shop. It is his favourite type of ice-cream – raspberry! Yummy!

How do you think Paul felt when he got his ice-cream?

_____

Circle the face which matches Paul's feeling:

Write down a time when you have felt like Paul:

_____

Rate your Feelings on the Feelometer:

_____

What did you say or do when you felt like Paul?

_____

_____

_____

Take Action

A Story from Dulcy

Dulcy thinks that being more aware in anxious situations is a great idea. Remember how Dulcy felt scared about her teacher Mrs Seahorse's loud voice when she was going to her swimming lesson?

In the future, Dulcy can be more aware by scanning her body to see if there have been any changes, like a fast beating heart. Dulcy can then decide whether it is a dangerous situation, or whether her body has set off a 'false alarm'. Dulcy can also scan the faces of the other sea animals around her to see how they are feeling about the swimming lesson. She can use the Feelometer to work out how anxious she is feeling.

Dulcy is going to take ACTION at her next swimming lesson, and she thinks it will be fun and safe.

Activity

Dulcy would like to ask you what you have learnt during the Be AWARE step.

Write down your answers on the lines below.

_____

_____

_____

_____

_____

C Step Two

I can keep CALM by doing On the Spot Deep Breathing and Move My Muscles Relaxation.

The first way to keep CALM is to practise On the Spot Deep Breathing.

On the Spot Deep Breathing can be used whenever you feel anxious and no one has to know you are doing it. That's why it's called "on the spot" deep breathing! Deep breathing helps you to stay CALM and not let your Anxious Body Signals bother you.

Let's see how it works:

1. Place one hand on your stomach and one hand on your chest. Imagine you have a balloon in your stomach and you want to blow it up really big. This means you have to push the air you breathe in all the way down into your stomach.

2. Slowly breathe in through your nose, counting to 3 and "blow up the balloon" in your stomach (make it big like the balloon above). Your chest should not move, only your stomach. Watch to see that only your hand on your stomach goes up as you "fill the balloon with air".

3. Hold your breath while you keep the balloon filled with air and say **Relax** to yourself.

4. Slowly breathe out through your nose counting to 3. The balloon in your stomach will get smaller when you breathe out, and the hand on your stomach should go down.

5. Hold your breath and say **Relax** to yourself.

> Each time you practise your Breathing blow the balloon UP and DOWN in your stomach at least 5 times.

Activity
Using On the Spot Deep Breathing

Write down when you could use On the Spot Deep Breathing to keep CALM on the lines below:

_____

_____

The second way to keep CALM is to practise Move My Muscles Relaxation.

Relaxation works really well in getting rid of the tightness in your muscles. In this relaxation exercise, you tense and then relax muscles from your face to your feet.

Let's see how it works:

1. **FACE:** Screw up your face (including your nose and eyes) and count to 3. Pretend that you have just smelt something really bad. Then say **Relax** to yourself and relax your face.

2. **SHOULDERS:** Shrug your shoulders upwards — try to make them touch your ears — and count to 3. Then say **Relax** to yourself and drop your shoulders down again.

3. **HANDS:** Squeeze your fingers together, like you are squeezing a ball and count to 3. Then say **Relax** to yourself and let your fingers open up.

4. **STOMACH:** Pull your stomach in and pretend you are trying to squeeze through a very small gap. Count to 3. Then say **Relax** to yourself and push your stomach out again.

5. **LEGS:** Make your legs really straight and tighten all the muscles in your legs. Count to 3. Then say **Relax** to yourself and make your legs all floppy (like a rag doll).

6. **FEET:** Clench and point your toes towards the floor. Count to 3. Then say **Relax** to yourself, roll your feet around in circles, and relax your toes

Activity
Move My Muscles Relaxation

Write down when you could use Move My Muscles Relaxation to keep CALM:

_____

_____

Take Action

Move My Muscles Relaxation Cards

1. FACE:

Screw up your face (including your nose and eyes) and count to 3. Pretend that you have just smelt something really bad. Then say **Relax** to yourself and relax your face.

2. SHOULDERS:

Shrug your shoulders upwards — try to make them touch your ears — and count to 3. Then say **Relax** to yourself and drop your shoulders down again.

3. HANDS:

Squeeze your fingers together, like you are squeezing a ball and count to 3. Then say **Relax** to yourself and let your fingers open up.

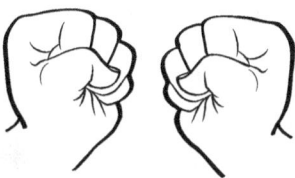

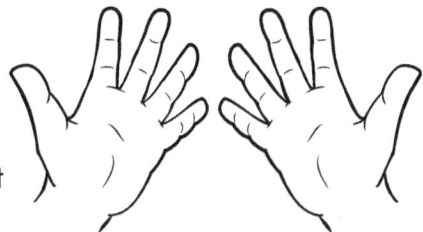

Take Action

4. STOMACH:

Pull your stomach in and pretend you are trying to squeeze through a very small gap. Count to 3. Then say **Relax** to yourself and push your stomach out again.

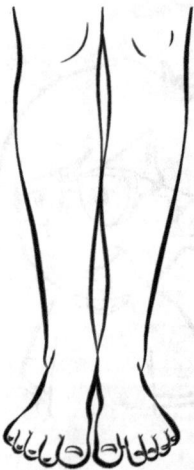

5. LEGS:

Make your legs really straight and tighten all the muscles in your legs. Count to 3. Then say **Relax** to yourself and make your legs all floppy (like a rag doll).

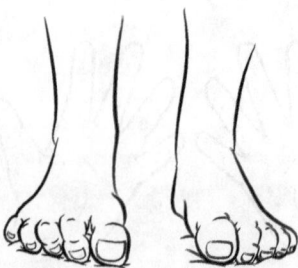

6. FEET:

Clench and point your toes towards the floor. Count to 3. Then say **Relax** to yourself, roll your feet around in circles, and unclench your toes.

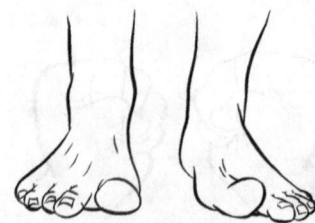

Congratulations! You have learnt two ways to keep CALM. Practise your On the Spot Deep Breathing and Muscle Relaxation whenever you are AWARE of feeling anxious!

A Story from Dion

Dion can see that you have learnt about how to be AWARE of your Anxious Body Signals and different feelings shown on our faces. You can now use the Feelometer to help work out how anxious you are feeling. You also learnt about ways to keep CALM. Dion liked the On the Spot Deep Breathing and he is going to use this to help keep himself CALM in scary situations. It is also a good idea to keep your muscles relaxed so it is easier to take ACTION against anxiety. Dion thinks that learning how to keep CALM is like learning how to play a new computer game. If you practise every day, you will get really good at it.

Activity

Dion would like to ask you what you have learnt during the Keep CALM step.

Write down your answers on the lines below:

_____

_____

_____

Activity
Planning for your Home Task

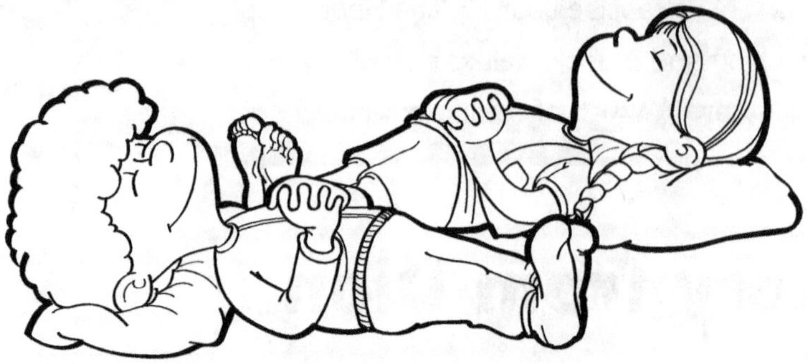

Your Home Task is to practise On the Spot Deep Breathing and Move My Muscles Relaxation every day. First let's do some planning so your Home Task is easy to finish.

1. Circle what time each day you will practise On the Spot Deep Breathing (you can circle more than one time):

   Morning   During the day   Afternoon   Night Time

2. Circle what time you will practise Move My Muscles Relaxation:

   Morning   During the day   Afternoon   Night Time

3. Think about what might stop you from doing your Breathing and Relaxation practice. Write down the things that might stop you from doing your Breathing and Relaxation on the lines below:

   ____

   ____

   ____

4. Write down how you can make sure that you practise your Breathing and Relaxation on the lines below:

   ____

   ____

   ____

T Step Three
I can THINK Strong Thoughts

Do you know that your thoughts are different to your feelings?

Thoughts come from inside your head. As Dulcy was going to school, she had two different thoughts:

It is a lovely day today.

I hope that my friend is at school today

We have talked about feelings like happy, angry, sad and anxious. Thoughts have a very powerful effect on Feelings and what you Do:

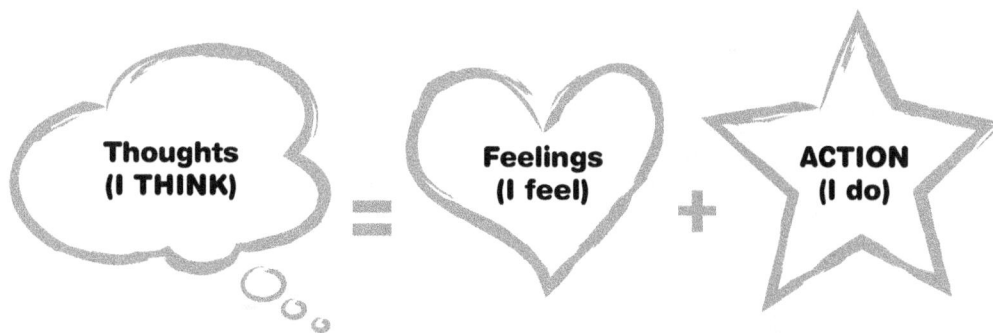

Thoughts (I THINK) = **Feelings (I feel)** + **ACTION (I do)**

The way you THINK can change how you feel and what you do because your thoughts always come first!

Activity
It's all about how we THINK

Let's learn more about thoughts and how they can change the way you feel and what you do.

Three animals are going to their first swimming lesson in the ocean. The animals are good at swimming in the pool, but this is the first time they have swum in the ocean. Each animal thinks about swimming in the ocean in a different way. Write down the feeling you THINK each animal would have because of their thoughts.

I don't want to go swimming in the ocean! Something bad will happen to me!

How might Dianne the Duck be feeling?

_____

How might Freddie the Fish be feeling?

He better not be making fun of how I swim!

_____

Hurray, we finally get to go swimming in the ocean. I can't wait to see all the pretty coral in the ocean.

How might Sammy the Starfish be feeling?

_____

If you THINK Scared Thoughts, you will feel scared and you will miss out on things that might be fun if you tried them!

Take Action

Activity
What you THINK is what you feel and do

THINK of a time when you felt anxious like Dianne the Duck.
Write your answers on the lines below:

I felt anxious when _____

Rate your Feelings on the Feelometer:_____

What did you THINK about when you felt anxious?_____

What did you DO when you felt anxious?_____

_____

THINK of a time when you felt angry like Freddie the Fish.
Write your answers on the lines below:

I felt angry when _____

Rate your Feelings on the Feelometer: _____

What did you THINK about when you felt angry?_____

What did you DO when you felt angry?_____

_____

THINK of a time when you felt happy like Sammy the Starfish.
Write your answers on the lines below:

I felt happy when_____

Rate your Feelings on the Feelometer:_____

What did you THINK about when you felt happy?_____

What did you DO when you felt happy?_____

_____

Take Action

We all THINK about things differently

Dulcy and Dion saw their friend Stuart the Seal and they both waved to him. Stuart did not wave back to them. Dulcy and Dion had different thoughts about this situation:

Stuart didn't wave to us. He must not like me any more. I'll never talk to him again.

Stuart didn't wave back – maybe he did not see us. I'll call out his name to get his attention.

Activity
Answer the questions on the lines below

How would Dulcy's thoughts make her feel? _____

What might Dulcy's actions be? _____

How would Dion's thoughts make him feel? _____

What might Dion's actions be? _____

_____

_____

We can THINK about the same situation in different ways. Scared thoughts make children feel anxious, get Anxious Body Signals and do things that are not helpful (like Dulcy saying she will never talk to Stuart again)

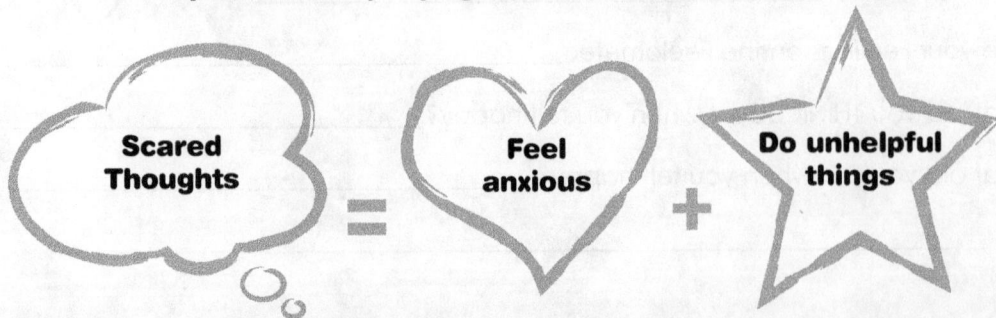

Scared Thoughts = **Feel anxious** + **Do unhelpful things**

Scared Thoughts

I was scared at that place last time – I can't go back there.

I'm never going to be able to do it.

- **Scared Thoughts** make you feel anxious (or Hot on the Feelometer) when you could feel Cool and relaxed.

- **Scared Thoughts** send off 'false alarms' and give you Anxious Body Signals, like a fast beating heart.

- **Scared Thoughts** are unhelpful and make children miss out on fun things because they are too scared to try them.

Catching thoughts by being AWARE of Anxious Body Signals

Thoughts (I THINK) = **Feelings (I feel)** + **ACTION (I do)**

You can catch Scared Thoughts by being AWARE of your Anxious Body Signals.

Activity
THINK of a time when you felt anxious.

I felt anxious when _____

Rate your Feelings on the Feelometer: _____

What Anxious Body Signals do you remember having? _____
_____
_____

What made you feel scared in that situation? _____
_____
_____

What did you think was going to happen in that situation? _____
_____

What did you do when you felt anxious in that situation? _____
_____
_____

Take Action

Activity
Catching thoughts by being AWARE

Look at this picture and write down your answers below to practise being AWARE of your thoughts:

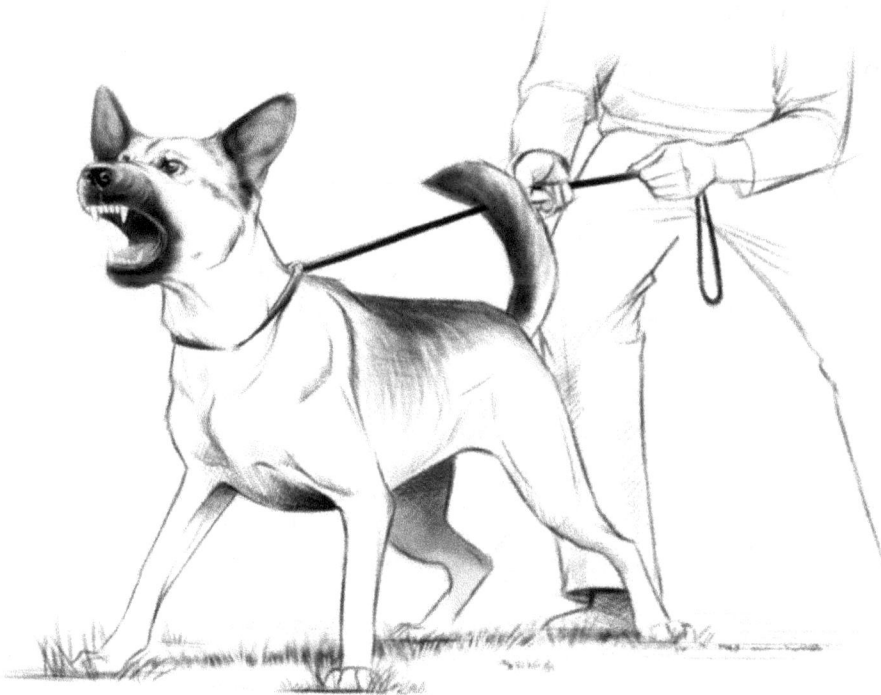

Rate your Feelings on the Feelometer: _____

What Anxious Body Signals do you notice having? _____

_____

What thoughts come to mind? _____

_____

What do you think would happen in this situation? _____

_____

Write down any other thoughts you noticed having:

_____

_____

_____

Activity
Catching thoughts by rewinding your mind!

THINK about your favourite sportsperson or celebrity.

Write down the person's name:

_____

Now THINK about this person in great detail. THINK about what they look like, what they do, and what their best performance has been.

Pretend your mind is like a DVD — rewind it back to when you first started thinking about your favourite person and remember what you were thinking. This is what you can do to catch thoughts when you are AWARE that you feel anxious. You can ask yourself "what was I just thinking about?" and then "play back" the situation in your mind to catch your thoughts. Tell the person next to you everything that you thought of about this sportsperson or celebrity.

Once you have caught your Scared Thoughts, you can swap them with Strong and Helpful Thoughts!

Strong Thoughts

I might feel scared now, but if I give it a try, I'll find out it's not that bad.

I can do this, I'll do my best!

- **Strong Thoughts** help you when you feel anxious.

- **Strong Thoughts** make you feel Cool and relaxed, instead of Hot on the Feelometer.

- **Strong Thoughts** help you to find out that the things you fear are not so scary, that they can be fun, and you can cope!

Strong Thoughts make you feel Strong, they are like big muscles that can help you take ACTION against anxiety!

Activity
Finding Strong Thoughts:
How Likely Is That?

My teacher is frowning. You think "He is angry at me".
But ask yourself "How likely is that?"

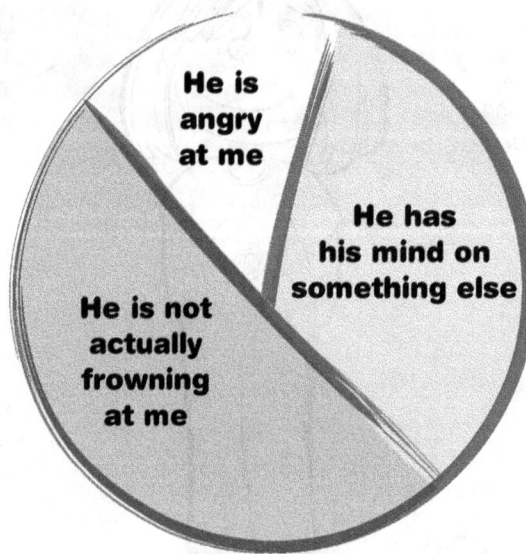

He is
angry
at me

He has
his mind on
something else

He is not
actually
frowning
at me

Thoughts	He is angry at me	He has his mind on something else	He is not actually frowning at me
Clues this is true	He is frowning	He was just talking on the phone before	He is looking at the other children being noisy
Clues this is false	He is not looking at me. I have done all my work	He is looking at the other children being noisy	He smiled at me a few minutes ago
Tick the most likely	✗	✗	✔

Take Action

Activity
Finding Your Strong Thoughts: How Likely Is That?

Think of a scary time and write your Scared Thought in one piece of the pie graph below. Ask yourself "HOW LIKELY IS THAT?" Then think of two other thoughts and fill in the table below to work out the most likely thought.

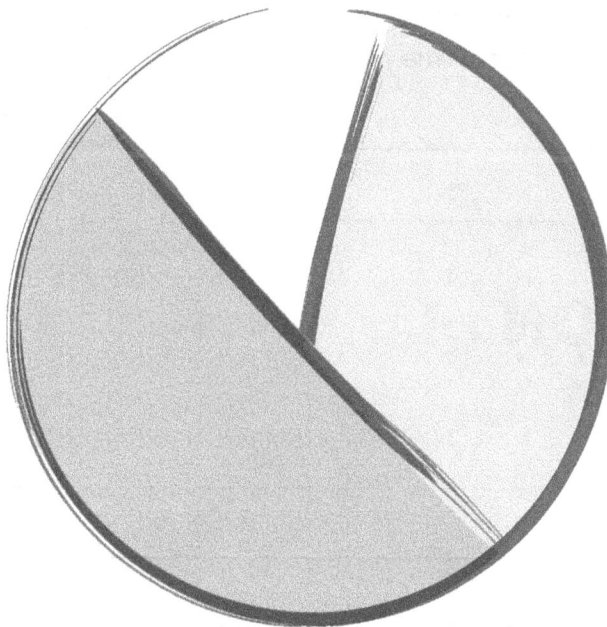

Thoughts			
Clues this is true			
Clues this is false			
Tick the most likely			

Take Action

Activity
Finding Strong Thoughts:
I Can Cope!

Sometimes situations can be a bit scary or uncomfortable (like going to the doctor or dentist). At these times, Strong Thoughts need to focus on coping ("I can do it"; "keep CALM")! What might be a scary time for you?

_____

_____

My ACTION plan

I will Keep CALM by:

_____

_____

_____

Strong Thoughts

My Strong Thoughts are:

_____

_____

_____

Take Action

Activity

Finding Strong Thoughts: Think of all the Options

Some children find speaking in front of the class really scary. They worry that other kids will laugh at them. When you feel anxious about a situation, you might THINK that the Scared Thought is true.

BUT there is always more than one Option in any situation.

Can you THINK of any other things that could happen if you had to speak in front of the class? Write all the possible options (both Scared and Strong Thoughts) you can THINK of in the thought bubbles below. Circle whether each option you have written down is a Scared or Strong Thought.

What is the best option to THINK in this situation? _____

Remember: Scared Thoughts are only thoughts! You can find a Strong Thought in every situation. A Strong Thought is always the best option!

Keeping Strong Thoughts: Strength Sayings

It is helpful to use catchy Strength Sayings to remember Strong Thoughts. Circle Strength Sayings below that might help you to keep focusing on Strong Thoughts.

(1) "How likely is that?" or (2) "What's the chances?"
These Strength Sayings help you to look for clues of how likely a Scared thought is and to find other options.

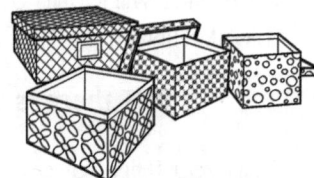

(3) "One step at a time" or (4) "Keep CALM" or (5) "I can do it"
These Strength Sayings remind you that you can cope and to keep trying, even if it feels hard.

(6) "Thoughts are just thoughts"
Our brains are like clever computers — they can think up all sorts of things. Saying to yourself "thoughts are just thoughts" reminds you not to be frightened or worried about thoughts. After all, a "thought is just a thought!"

(7) "In one ear and out the other"
This Strength Saying reminds you that you don't have to focus on every thought you have. You can imagine the thought going in one ear and floating out the other side!

(8) "Keep or Sweep?" or (9) "Throw it away!"
These Strength Sayings remind you that you can decide to keep Strong thoughts and discard Scary thoughts.

(10) "Keep your mind where your body is!"
Sometimes your mind can race ahead and you might worry about things in the future. This can make it hard to concentrate on what you are doing at the time. Saying to yourself 'keep your mind where your body is" can help bring your thoughts back to what you are doing.

(11) "Let it go!"
You could use this Strength Saying when you catch a Scary Thought or find yourself thinking about something over and over, like when you might be worrying about something.

(12) "Bring it on!"
You might use this Strength Saying when you have to do something that's a bit hard or uncomfortable but you have to do it (e.g., get a vaccination). This Strength Saying reminds you to take Action.

(13) "Do the opposite!"
You might catch a Scared Thought that tells you to avoid something. You could say to yourself "Do the opposite" and you might find out the situation wasn't as bad as you thought, and that you could handle it.

Keeping Strong Thoughts: Strength Cards

Dion has just realised that he has been worrying about being late for his swimming class. He noticed he had some Anxious Body Signals, like a fast beating heart and he felt sick in his stomach. Once he noticed these Anxious Body Signals, he was able to catch his Scared Thought. Dion thought about all his OPTIONS in this situation and came up with a Strong Thought (see below)

I will be late and it will be so bad – I'll get into trouble.

Scared Thought

I have everything ready. I will be on time

Strong Thought

Dion did a great job in finding a Strong Thought to weaken his Scared Thought. His Anxious Body Signals went away after thinking the Strong Thought and doing On the Spot Deep Breathing. Dion is going to make a Strength Card to strengthen his Strong Thoughts more.

Strength Cards

Strength Cards can help remind you of Strong Thoughts. On one side of a Strength Card, you write the Scared Thought that you are trying to weaken. On the other side of the Strength Card, you write the Strong Thought that you want to keep thinking.

SIDE 1 **Scared Thought**

I will be late
and it will be so bad –
I'll get into trouble.

SIDE 2 **Strong Thought**

I have
everything ready.
I will be on time.

Dion is going to keep his Strength Card with him during the day so that he can keep reminding himself of his Strong Thought

Step Four
I can Get INTO ACTION by climbing the steps of my ACTION Ladder and rewarding myself.

Dulcy started Grade 4 this year but she is having lots of trouble going to school. She is really afraid of swimming to school by herself. Her home is only 30 metres from her school but she can't go to school without her mum swimming with her. Dulcy wants to be able to swim to school by herself, like the other sea animals can — this is one of her Take ACTION Goals.

Dulcy has created an ACTION Ladder for swimming to school (see below). She has broken down her goal of swimming to school by herself into four smaller steps. These make up the steps in her ACTION Ladder and this will help her to take ACTION slowly, one step at a time. The first step is the smallest and easiest — it must be something that she knows she can do. Each step gets bigger but she will only move onto the next step when she feels CALM and relaxed (Cool on the Feelometer). Dulcy has to remember to use the skills in the ACTION plan — be AWARE of her Anxious Feelings and Body Signals, keep CALM by doing her Breathing and Relaxation and THINK Strong Thoughts — while she climbs the ACTION Ladder.

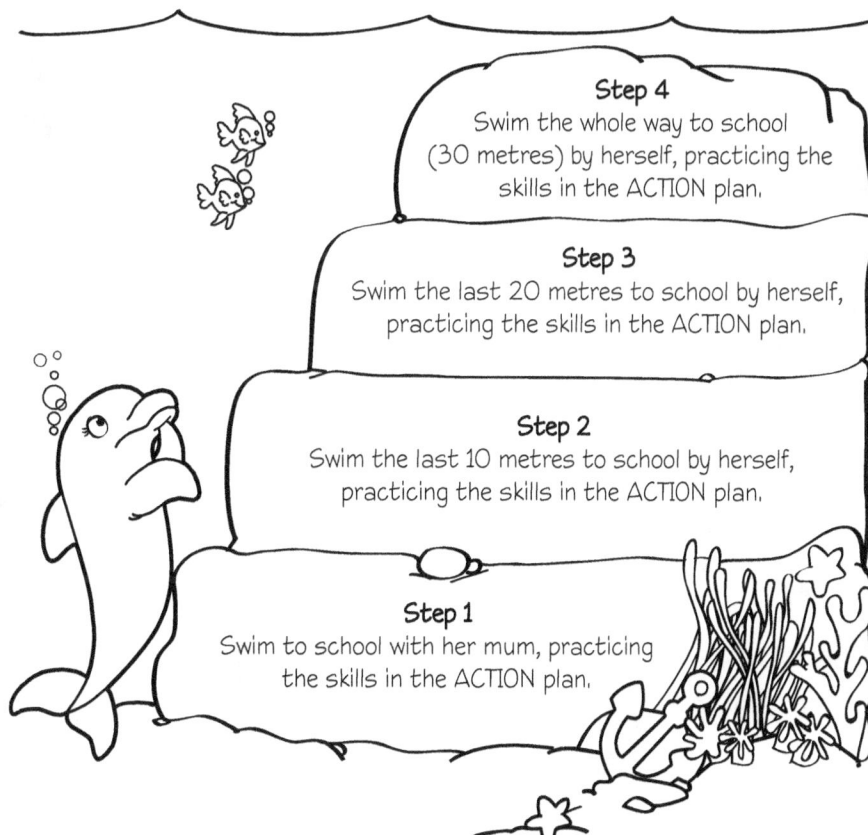

Step 4
Swim the whole way to school (30 metres) by herself, practicing the skills in the ACTION plan.

Step 3
Swim the last 20 metres to school by herself, practicing the skills in the ACTION plan.

Step 2
Swim the last 10 metres to school by herself, practicing the skills in the ACTION plan.

Step 1
Swim to school with her mum, practicing the skills in the ACTION plan.

Activity
Practise Makes Perfect

Practise identifying steps you could work towards for one of your Take ACTION goals. You can add more steps to the top if you need to.

Step 5

Step 4

Step 3

Step 2

Step 1

Take Action

Activity
My First Take ACTION Ladder

My Take ACTION Goal: _____

Write each smaller Goal and your Reward (★) in each Step below, starting at Step 1 which is the easiest and then working up the Steps.

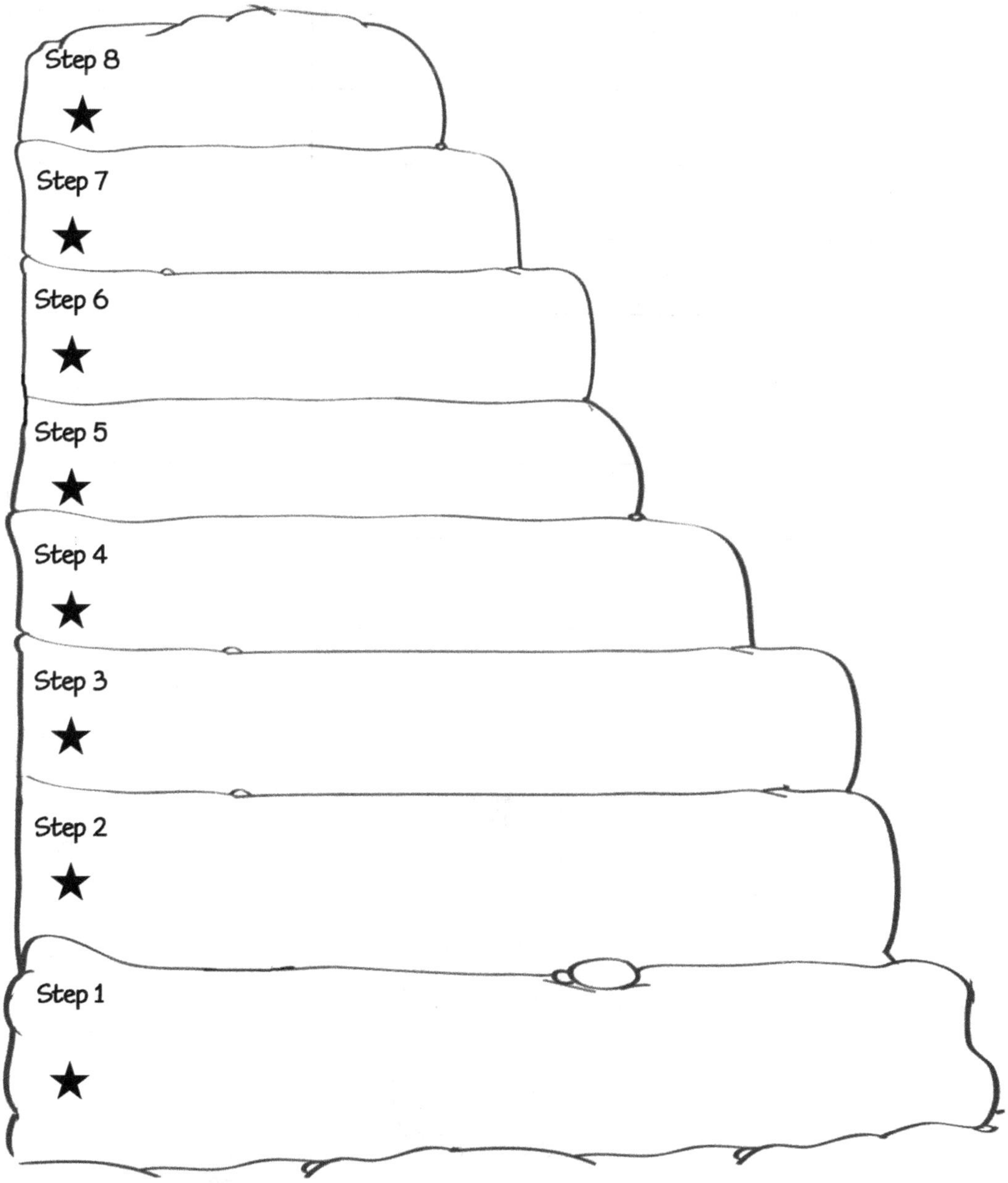

Step 8

★

Step 7

★

Step 6

★

Step 5

★

Step 4

★

Step 3

★

Step 2

★

Step 1

★

Take Action

Activity
Small steps towards my
First ACTION Ladder

My Take ACTION Goal for My Ladder _____

_____

Step on the ACTION Ladder	Fear (0-8)	Rank the steps

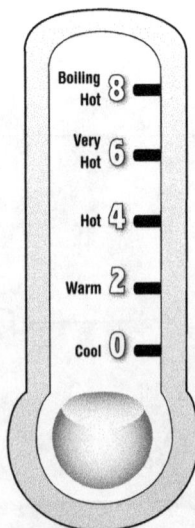

Boiling Hot 8

Very Hot 6

Hot 4

Warm 2

Cool 0

Activity
Small rewards towards my First ACTION Ladder

THINK of how you could reward yourself for climbing the steps on your ACTION Ladder. Remember rewards are not only money or other material things. Rewards can be things that you like to do (e.g., special outings) or things that make you feel good (e.g., playing on the computer) or even telling yourself you've done a good job. Write some possible rewards in the stars below:

Reward:

Reward:

Reward:

Reward:

Reward:

Reward:

ⓄStep Five

I can use my OPTIONS including Problem Solving, Strong Team, and to Focus on the Positives.

The first OPTION is Problem Solving

Dion wants to go to his friend's birthday party but he is worried no one will talk to him. One way he can solve this problem is to think of other OPTIONS and look at the ACTION he would take for each one to decide what is the best solution.

1. Thought OPTIONS List two thoughts you could have about this scary time.	**2. What type of thought is this (Scared; Strong)?**	**3. What ACTION would you take if you thought this way?**

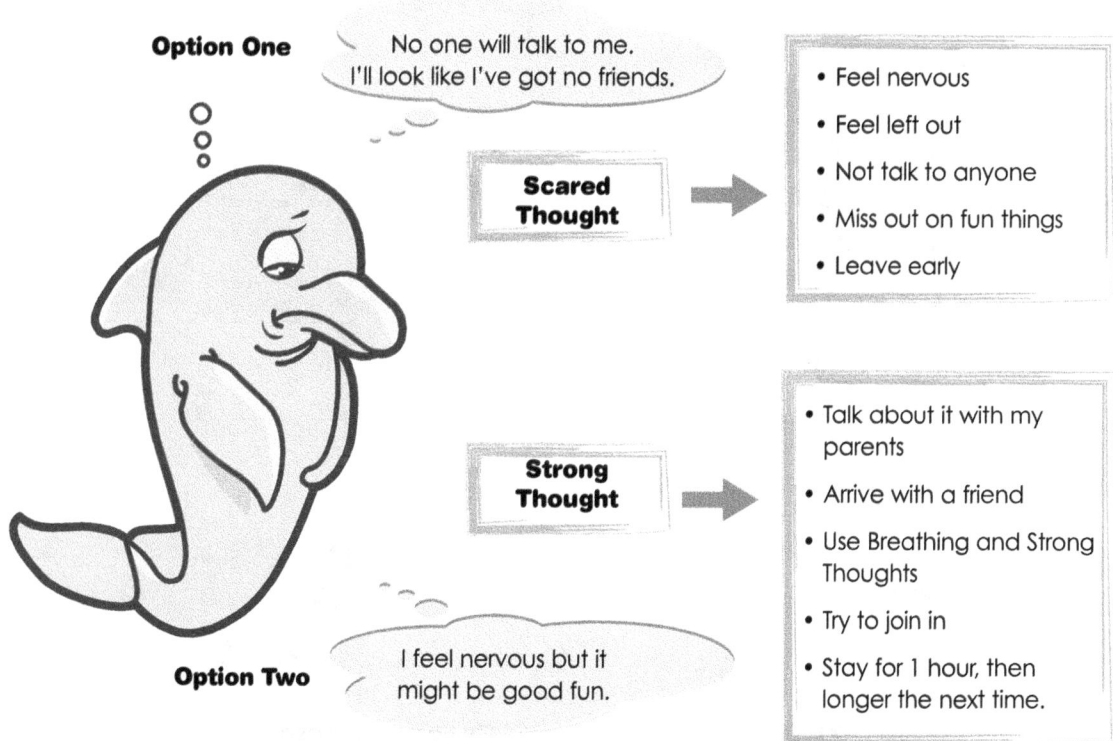

Option One

No one will talk to me. I'll look like I've got no friends.

Scared Thought ➡

- Feel nervous
- Feel left out
- Not talk to anyone
- Miss out on fun things
- Leave early

Strong Thought ➡

- Talk about it with my parents
- Arrive with a friend
- Use Breathing and Strong Thoughts
- Try to join in
- Stay for 1 hour, then longer the next time.

Option Two

I feel nervous but it might be good fun.

4. Weigh up the OPTIONS — What is the best Option for Dion to choose (Look at the ACTION column to decide)? _____

_____

5. Take ACTION — Dion does what he has listed in the ACTION column of the Strong Thought Option.

Activity
Problem Solving Practice

THINK about a scary time that you have had recently. Write the scary time in Option One below. Find another solution by thinking of a Strong OPTION and then weighing up the ACTION you would take for each one. Which is best?

1. Thought OPTIONS
List two thoughts you could have about this scary time.

2. What type of thought is this (Scared; Strong)?

3. What ACTION would you take if you thought this way?

Option One

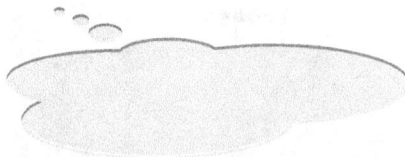

Option Two

4. Weigh up the OPTIONS — What is the best Option to choose (Look at the ACTION column to decide)? _____

_____

5. Take ACTION — Do what you have listed in the ACTION column of the Strong Thought Option

The second OPTION is a Strong Team

A Strong Team is a list of people who can help you to feel Strong and take ACTION against your anxiety. Strong Team members are positive people who can remind you of the skills in the ACTION plan.

Activity
Think of people that could be on your Strong Team.

Choose people from home (e.g., parents), school (e.g., teacher) and other areas of your life (e.g., sporting coach) so you can always have a Strong Team member close by. Write your Strong Team members on the lines below.

My Strong Team members are:

1._____

2._____

3._____

4._____

5._____

What situations could your Strong Team members help you with?

_____

_____

What could your Strong Team members do to help you (e.g., listen to you, remind you of the skills in the ACTION plan)?

_____

_____

Ask the people you listed above if they will be part of your Strong Team. Tell your Strong Team members what situations they can help you with, and how they can best help you to take ACTION against anxiety.

The third OPTION is to Focus on the Positives

Remember from the "THINK Strong Thoughts" Module that Strength Sayings are catchy sayings that will help you to feel Strong as you are taking ACTION against anxiety.

Some examples of Strength Sayings are:

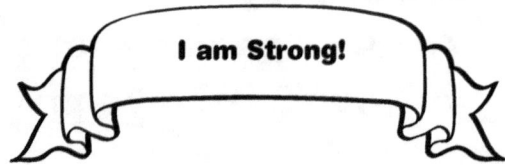

I can do it!

I am Strong!

Activity

Now that you have more experience feeling strong by doing your ACTION Ladder, think about some more Strength Sayings that you can use to keep feeling Strong.

Write your Strength Sayings in the ribbons below:

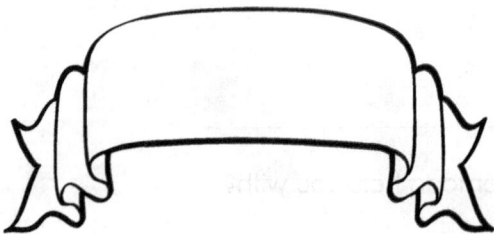

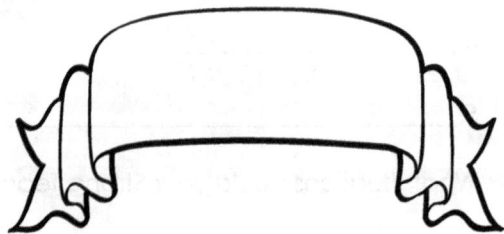

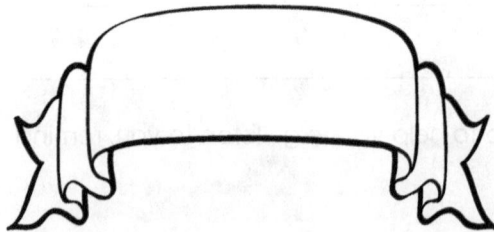

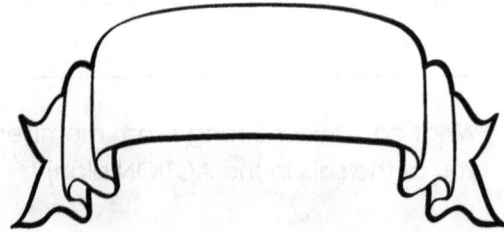

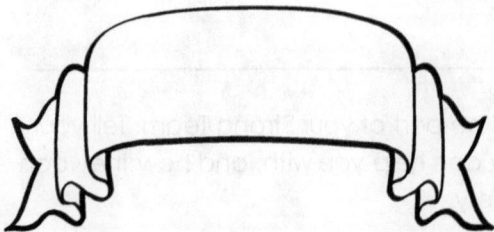

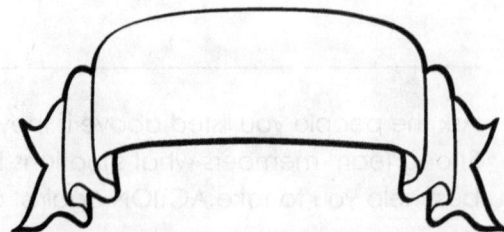

Keep Being Positive

Here are helpful things you can do to keep Being Positive:

Keep your body active and try new things!

Smile a lot!

Think about nice things you enjoy!

Believe in yourself and never give up!

Keep doing these things so you Feel Strong like Dulcy and Dion.

Activity
Things I can do well

Try to list as many positive things about yourself as possible. These can be things you do well (e.g., I'm a good swimmer) or things you like about yourself (e.g., I'm friendly towards other people). Try to be creative and list EVERYTHING you can think of.

Activity
Things I like about me

A Story from Dulcy

Dulcy can see that you have learnt three more OPTIONS so far to use when taking ACTION against anxiety. The first Option is Problem Solving, which helps you to find the best Option to deal with a scary time. The second Option is a Strong Team that is full of people who can help remind you of the skills in the ACTION plan. The third Option is to Focus on the Positives. Strength Sayings will help you feel Strong when you are taking ACTION. It is also important to focus on the good things about yourself, other people and the world around you. Remind yourself of the things you do well and what you like about yourself. Dulcy thinks that using all these OPTIONS will help you take ACTION and feel happy.

Activity

Dulcy would like to ask you what you have learnt so far during the Use My OPTIONS step

Write down your answers on the lines below:

_____

_____

_____

_____

_____

_____

The fourth OPTION is having Confident Body Signals

Children who get anxious often find it hard to talk to other people and stand up for themselves, and they might get bullied. Showing Confident Body Signals can help you to be confident, assertive and deal with bullies.

Remember back to when you learnt about Anxious Body Signals (e.g. fast beating heart). You now know how to keep CALM (by using On the Spot Deep Breathing and Move my Muscles Relaxation) to reduce these Anxious Body Signals.

Confident Body Signals help you to look Confident in social situations (e.g. talking with a friend at school). There is an easy way to remember your Strong Confident Body Signals — just remember to:

SMILE

S Smile and face the other person.

M MAKE eye contact and look interested while you are talking with the other person.

I INITIATE the conversation.
Remember to:
- Use a greeting (e.g., "Hello") when introducing yourself
- Pick a topic that you both like to talk about
- Ask questions

L LISTEN to the other person.

E ENJOY yourself and relax:
- Use On the Spot Deep Breathing
- Remember your Strength Sayings
- Keep smiling

Take ACTION Task One

Write down some good conversation topics on the lines below

_____

_____

_____

_____

Pick a topic to talk about with your partner. Practise using your Confident Body Signals (SMILE) while you talk about this topic.

How did you feel on the Feelometer before the Take ACTION Task?

_____

How did you feel on the Feelometer after the Take ACTION Task?

_____

How did your Confident Body Signals help you during the Take ACTION Task?

_____

_____

Start practising SMILE with your family and friends. Using Confident Body Signals will help you to look Confident and keep taking ACTION against anxiety!

The fifth OPTION is Being Confident and Assertive

Look at the three different ways that you can act towards other children and adults below.

The Shy Starfish Way

Whatever you say, I'll do

Acting like the Shy Starfish means you might ignore the situation or 'give in' to the other person. You do not say how you feel about the situation.

• **Feelings:** Shy, embarrassed, nervous, useless, unhappy.

• **Body Signals:** Talk softly like a mouse, mumble, look down at the floor, stand far away, hunch over, feel Hot on the Feelometer.

• **You might say things like:** "Whatever you say", "I don't know", "If you say so".

• **Actions:** You might do things like walk away, not be able to say NO, give the other person what they want (even if you don't want to!), avoid the problem, get upset.

Do you think that this is a good way to act?

☐ YES ☐ NO

The Angry Shark Way

You better do this for me or else...

Acting like the Angry Shark means you attack the other person, over-react or get angry at the other person.

- **Feelings:** Angry, annoyed, out of control, mean.

- **Body signals:** Stand close to the other person, look angry, have tight muscles and clenched fists, feel Hot on the Feelometer.

- **You might say things like:** "You'd better do this for me", "If you don't do this, watch out", "I want this now".

- **Actions:** You might do things like look angry, threaten, push, hit, kick, shout, yell, speak rudely or tease.

Do you think that this is a good way to act?

☐ YES   ☐ NO

The Strong Dolphin Way: Being Confident and Assertive

I would like to do it this way

Acting like the Strong Dolphin means you say how you feel and speak up for yourself in an honest, polite and friendly way. This is called being Assertive!

- **Feelings:** Happy, confident, in control and you feel good about yourself.

- **Body signals:** Stand tall, smile, look CALM, look others in the eyes, feel Cool on the Feelometer.

- **You might say things like:** "I THINK that…", "Let's try", "I would like to do it this way".

- **Actions:** You might do things like speak firmly but friendly, be confident and relaxed, listen to the other person's point of view, speak up for your rights, find a solution to the problem and make more friends.

Do you think that this is a good way to act?

☐ YES ☐ NO

Acting like the Strong Dolphin means you are being Confident and Assertive. This is the best way to act towards other people!

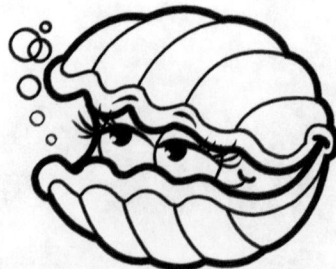

Three Steps to being Confident and Assertive

Dulcy would like to act in a Confident and Assertive way with her friend but she doesn't know how to. Dulcy's friend borrowed her swimming cap three weeks ago and she hasn't given it back to her. Dulcy really needs her swimming cap so she can keep climbing her ACTION Ladder of swimming to school by herself. Let's help Dulcy to be Confident and Assertive by following the steps below.

Step One: Tell the other person what you think the problem is

Sally, when you borrowed my swimming cap three weeks ago, I thought you would give it back to me after your lesson.

Step Two: Tell the other person how you feel about the problem

I feel annoyed that you haven't given my swimming cap back.

Step Three: Tell the other person a solution to the problem

I would really like it if you gave me my swimming cap back today.

Things to remember when being Confident and Assertive:
- Use your Confident Body Signals (SMILE).
- Keep CALM by doing On the Spot Deep Breathing
- THINK Strong Thoughts.
- Discuss the solution you have thought of with the other person. Remember to listen to their point of view as well!

Congratulate yourself if you tried to be Confident and Assertive!!

Take Action

Take ACTION Task Two

Read the two stories below. Write a Confident and Assertive way of acting following the three steps listed. After you have written down a Confident and Assertive response, role play each situation with a partner.

Story One

Your friend has been bossing you around at lunch time. You have decided you don't want to be bossed around anymore.

Step One: Tell the other person what you think the problem is

Step Two: Tell the other person how you feel about the problem

Step Three: Tell the other person a solution to the problem

Story Two

Your friend wants to copy answers from a Maths test you studied hard for.

Step One: Tell the other person what you think the problem is

Step Two: Tell the other person how you feel about the problem

Step Three: Tell the other person a solution to the problem

The sixth OPTION is learning the Steps for Dealing with Bullying.

There are different ways that children can be bullied. Some examples of bullying include:

- Being made fun of for something you said or did;

- Other kids saying mean things about you to others or to you;

- Someone teasing you about your looks or because you are different from them;

- Being left out of activities;

- Being physically hurt or your property damaged.

Why do children bully others?

- They think they are cool or powerful, but bullies are usually not confident themselves. They bully others to make themselves feel good.

- They might be jealous of something good about you.

- They are bored.

- They are trying to "push your buttons" and get a reaction – they want to be noticed or get attention.

If you react to the bullying, the bully gets what they want: a reaction.

It is helpful to deal with bullying by being Confident and Assertive (like you have learnt already) and following the steps for Dealing with Bullying.

Steps for Dealing with Bullying

Step One: Stop what you are doing and practise your On the Spot Deep Breathing. This will help you to keep CALM.

Step Two: THINK about the OPTIONS that you have in the situation. Some Strong and Confident OPTIONS to choose from are:

Walk away

Tell an adult

Ignore the bullying if you can

Say "I heard what you said and I don't really care"

Tell them firmly and calmly to leave you alone

Imagine there is a force field all around you protecting you from their words

Step Three: Decide on the best Option and take ACTION. Say how you feel in a Confident and Assertive way (like the Strong Dolphin).

Things to remember when Dealing with Bullying:

- Use your Confident Body Signals (SMILE).
- Keep CALM by doing On the Spot Deep Breathing.
- THINK Strong Thoughts.
- Do not yell or scream, call them names, or be physically aggressive.

Congratulate yourself for dealing with this situation!

Activity

Dion has been bullied by Shawn the Shark at school for the last few weeks. Shawn says things to Dion like:

> Hey Dion, you are scared all the time. Why can't you be tough like me?

Write down what Dion should do at each step for dealing with Shawn's bullying:

Step One: _____

Step Two: Circle which Strong and Confident OPTIONS Dion should choose.

Walk away

Tell an adult

Ignore the bullying if you can

Say "I heard what you said and I don't really care"

Tell them firmly and calmly to leave you alone

Imagine there is a force field all around you protecting you from their words

What is the best Option for Dion to choose? _____

Take ACTION Task Three

Role play the situation that you have just helped Dion with. Remember to follow the three Steps for Dealing with Bullying with your partner.

Do you think you could use these steps yourself if you are bullied in the future? Circle one of the boxes below.

Yes! I could use these steps!	**Yes! But I think I need a bit more practice!**

If the bullying keeps going talk to your parents, and your teacher if it happened at school. You could also talk to your Strong Team members to work out a plan of ACTION.

Story from Dulcy

Dulcy can see that you have learnt three more OPTIONS to use in your ACTION Plan. Using Confident Body Signals (SMILE); being Confident and Assertive (like the Strong Dolphin) with other children and adults; and learning the Steps for Dealing with Bullying will help you to keep taking ACTION against situations that worry you. Dulcy thinks that if you keep taking ACTION against anxiety, you will learn that you are a Strong and Confident person. You will be able to enjoy things more and be happy. Keep up the great work!

Activity

Dulcy would like to ask you what you have learnt during the Use My OPTIONS step.

"Write down your answers on the lines below.

_____

_____

N Step Six
I will NEVER stop taking ACTION against anxiety

You have done a great job learning to Take ACTION against anxiety

You have learnt six steps in the ACTION plan to help you deal with anxiety. It is important that you NEVER stop taking ACTION in the future.

By planning for times in the future when you may need your ACTION plan, you will already be prepared and Strong!

Activity

For each of the six steps in the ACTION plan, write down the skills that will help you take ACTION against anxiety in the future.

Be AWARE
_____

Keep CALM
_____

THINK Strong Thoughts
_____

Get INTO Action
_____

Use my OPTIONS
_____

NEVER stop taking ACTION
_____

Let's put the steps into ACTION — Jack's Story

Jack feels anxious about going to school. Here's how he took ACTION to overcome his fears.

A — Be AWARE

When I wake up in the morning, I am AWARE that I am feeling anxious. I have Anxious Body Signals like butterflies in my stomach and a fast beating heart. I would rate myself as Boiling Hot on the Feelometer.

C — Keep CALM

I use my Move my Muscles Relaxation while I am lying in bed to get calmer. I feel much better after I tense and relax my face, shoulders, hands, stomach, legs and feet. While I am getting ready for school, I use my On the Spot Deep Breathing. When I slowly breathe in and out, I feel more relaxed. I can also use my Breathing at school if I start to feel anxious.

T — THINK Strong Thoughts

I THINK Strong Thoughts, like "I don't need to be anxious, I have my favourite lesson today". I will take the Strength Card that I made for this scary time and keep it in my shorts pocket — that way I can look at it if I feel anxious. Thinking Strong Thoughts helps me to feel Strong and Confident.

I — Get INTO Action

I Get INTO Action to learn to feel calm going to school by using an ACTION Ladder (see over page). The steps on my ACTION ladder get bigger but I can take it slowly — one step at a time. I reward myself for taking ACTION on each step of the Ladder.

O — Use my OPTIONS

I have other OPTIONS to use when I feel anxious as well. I could say my favourite Strength Saying "I can do this" to myself. My mum reminds me to take ACTION — she is part of my Strong Team. I also use Problem Solving at school if I need to. I Keep Focusing on the Positives and be confident with other children by using SMILE and Being Assertive!

N — NEVER stop taking ACTION

I will NEVER stop taking ACTION against feeling anxious when I go to school. I know that sometimes it will be hard and sometimes it will be easy.
I can use all the skills in my Action Plan to Be AWARE, to Keep CALM, to THINK Strong Thoughts, to Get INTO Action and use all my OPTIONS. I know that I will enjoy school more and be happier if I keep taking ACTION.

Take Action

Jack's ACTION Ladder

I have to stay on each step of my ACTION Ladder until I feel CALM and relaxed (Cool on the Feelometer). If I have difficulty with any of the steps on my ACTION Ladder, I need to practise that step until I master it.

Step 4
Walk to the classroom by myself.
★ I will reward myself by ringing my Grandma overseas.

Step 3
Walk to the classroom by myself, with my friend waiting at the classroom. ★ I will reward myself by picking what my family has for dinner.

Step 2
Walk to my classroom with a friend.
★ I will reward myself by talking on the phone to my friend.

Step 1
Walk to my classroom with mum.
★ I will reward myself with my favourite ice-cream after school.

**You can make a story for your own scary times.
Remember to use all the steps in the ACTION plan when writing your story!**

Activity

Think back to when you first started the Take Action program and you were not feeling as Strong or Confident about facing anxiety.

Draw a picture or write some words in the box below that shows how you felt before you knew the steps in the ACTION plan.

Take Action

Activity

Now think about how you feel after completing the Take Action program. Think about the Take Action Goals that you have achieved.

Draw a picture or write some words in the box below that shows how Strong and Confident you feel because you now have an ACTION plan.

Things my therapist noticed about my progress during the Take Action Program.

Activity

Looking Ahead — NEVER Stop Taking ACTION

Think about scary times you still have now, or times in the future that you might find scary. An example of a future scary time might be starting a new grade at school. Knowing what some of these scary times might be means you can use your ACTION Plan when you need it! Write down some future scary times on the lines below.

Scary times might be: _____

_____

Activity

For each of the six steps in the ACTION plan, write down the skills that will help you take ACTION against anxiety in the future.

A _____

C _____

T _____

I _____

O _____

N _____

My ACTION Ladder

Talk with your parents about the scary times you have written down previously. Choose one of these scary times and create another ACTION Ladder.

My Take ACTION Goal _____

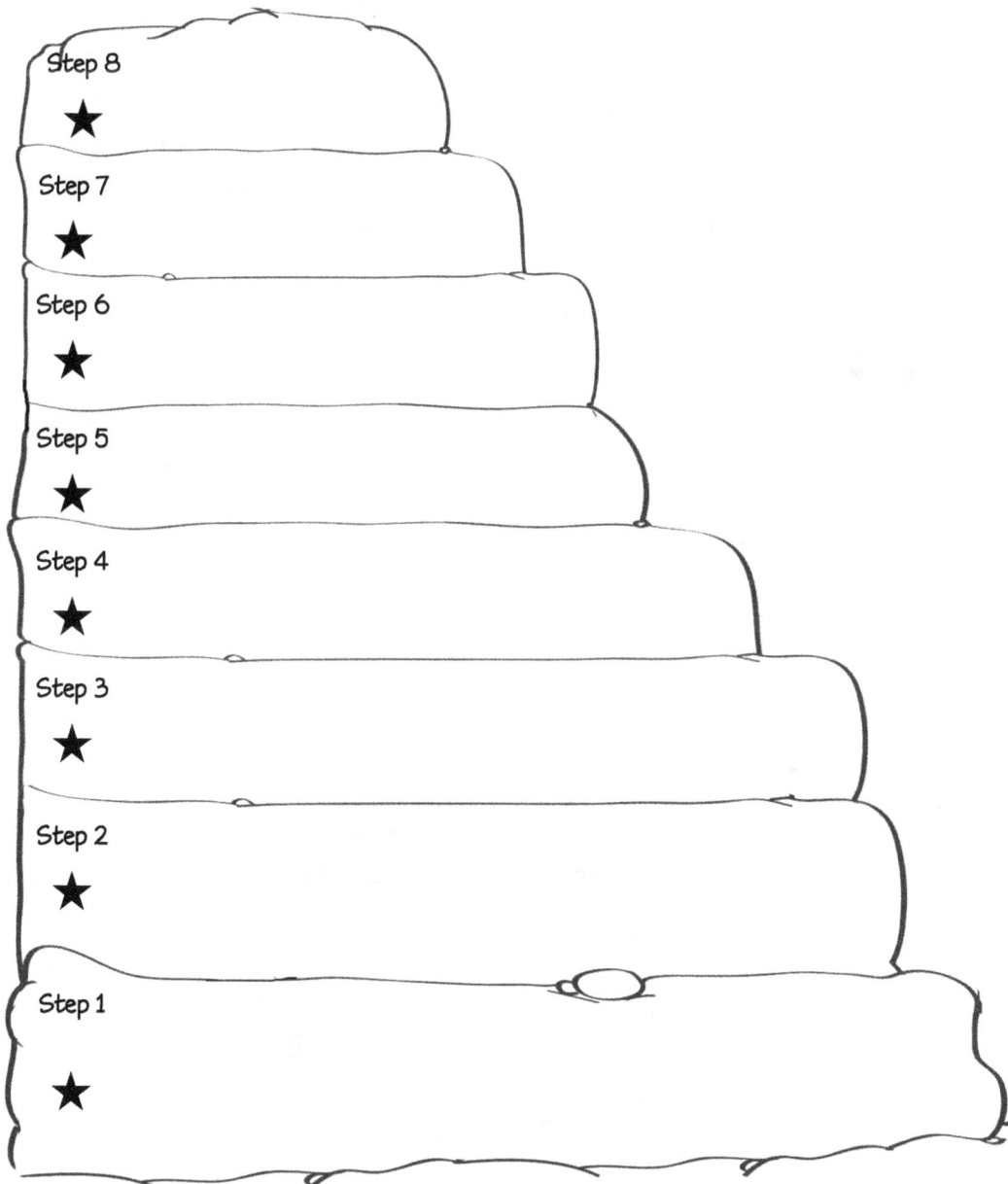

_____

Step 8

★

Step 7

★

Step 6

★

Step 5

★

Step 4

★

Step 3

★

Step 2

★

Step 1

★

A Story from Dulcy and Dion!

Dulcy and Dion can see you have learnt about how to keep taking ACTION in the future. Dulcy and Dion know that they have learnt a lot from the Take Action program and they hope you have too! Dulcy and Dion think you should put your Take ACTION bookmark and this workbook somewhere safe so that you can read about your ACTION plan whenever you need to. Dulcy and Dion have really enjoyed doing the Take Action program with you. Remember to NEVER stop taking ACTION in the future and your anxiety will stay away. Dulcy and Dion wish you all the best for the future and hope that you continue to be strong and happy!

Activity

Dulcy and Dion would like to ask you what you have learnt in the NEVER stop taking Action step. On the lines below, write down your answer.

During the NEVER stop taking Action step, I learnt

_____

_____

_____

Always remember: You can feel better about anything that scares or worries you by using your

ACTION

Plan!

Congratulations
to

....

on completing

The
Take Action
Program!

You now have an ACTION Plan
to use in the future whenever you
need to take ACTION against anxiety!

....
Practitioner's Signature   Date

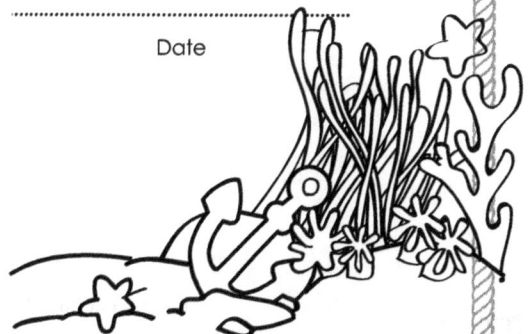

Home Task Reward Chart

Every time you complete a Home Task, you will receive a tick in the box that matches that week's Home Task. See if you can earn all the ticks by the end of the Take Action program.

Session	Home Tasks Assigned	Tick Completed	Therapist's Signature
1			
2	One, Two		
3	Three,		
4	Three, Four		
5	Three, Five		
6	Three, Six, Seven		
7	Three, Six, Seven		
8	Three, Six, Seven, Eight		
9	Three, Six, Seven, Eight, Nine		
10			

Home Task One
Rewards Menu

It is important that you are rewarded for doing your Home Tasks. Here's an example of a Reward Menu:

Home Task Number	Reward
1	10 minutes to spend on favourite activity
2	Favourite snack
3	20 minutes to spend on favourite activity
4	Getting your favourite dinner
5	Getting a stress ball
6	Getting a new writing book
7	Getting a new game
8	Going on a family picnic
9	Going to the movies
10	Trip to a theme park

Talk to your parents about what rewards you would like for completing your Home Tasks. Remember rewards are not only money or other material things. Rewards can be things that you like to do (e.g. special outings) or things that make you feel good (e.g. playing the computer) or even telling yourself you've done a good job.

Write down the rewards in the table below. Remember you will receive one tick each time you complete a Home Task. Ask your parent/s to sign underneath the Rewards Menu. You can earn smaller rewards throughout the program, or you can save your ticks for a larger reward (e.g. trip to a theme park after earning 10 ticks).

My Rewards Menu

Home Task Number	Reward
1	
2	
3	
4	
5	
6	
7	
8	
9	
10	

I agree with _____ (child's name) Reward Menu and will be able to provide these rewards for _____ (child's name)

Parent's Signature:
_____

Home Task Two

Write down a time that you felt each of the emotions below:

1. Happy or Excited

Rate your level on the Feelometer:

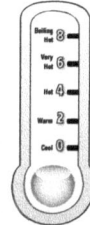

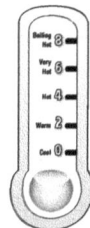

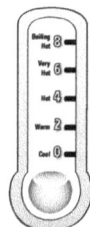

_____

How did you know that you felt happy or excited (e.g. I was smiling):

_____

2. Anxious

Rate your level on the Feelometer:

_____

How did you know that you felt anxious (e.g. my heart was beating fast):

_____

3. CALM and Relaxed

Rate your level on the Feelometer:

_____

How did you know that you felt calm and relaxed (e.g. I was laughing with my friends):

_____

_____

Home Task Three
On the Spot Deep Breathing and Move My Muscles Relaxation Practice

For each day of the week shown below, tick the box if you practised your Breathing and Relaxation. Write down your rating on the Feelometer before and after doing your Breathing and Relaxation (Sunday is practise-free!).

	Monday	Tuesday	Wednesday	Thursday	Friday	Saturday
Tick if you did your Deep Breathing						
Rating on Feelometer before Breathing						
Rating on Feelometer after Breathing						
Tick if you did your Muscle Relaxation						
Rating on Feelometer before Relaxation						
Rating on Feelometer after Relaxation						

Home Task Four
Catching Scared Thoughts

In this Home Task, catch some Scared Thoughts you had during the week and write them in the table below.

If you do not have any Scared Thoughts this week, THINK about scary times you have had over the past few weeks or months and then fill in the table.

	Example	My Scary Time	My Scary Time
What happened?	I had to give a talk in my class		
What Anxious Body Signals did you have?	Fast beating heart and butterflies in my stomach.		
How did you feel?	Scared		
Rating on the Feelometer	Boiling Hot		
What Scared Thoughts did you have?	The other kids will laugh at me. I will forget what I have to say.		
What ACTION did you take?	I told my mum that I felt sick so I didn't have to go to school		

This page is intentionally blank.

Take Action

Home Task Five
Strength Cards

THINK of a Scared Thought you have had recently.

What was the Scared Thought you had? _____

_____

How did the Scared Thought make you feel? _____

_____

What Anxious Body Signals did you have? _____

_____

Rating on the Feelometer: _____

Write the Scared Thought on Side 1 of your Strength Card.

SIDE 1 **Scared Thought**

THINK of a Strong Thought that you can use to weaken the Scared Thought.
Write the Strong Thought on Side 2 of your Strength Card.

SIDE 2 **Strong Thought**

This page is intentionally blank.

Home Task Six
Reviewing my ACTION Plan

Let's review how things went while you completed a step on your ACTION Ladder. Remember to use all the skills in the ACTION plan while you are practising each step.

Write down the step on your ACTION Ladder on the lines below.

_____

_____

A

Be AWARE:

How did you feel before doing this step on your ACTION Ladder?

What Anxious Body Signals did you have? _____

_____

Rating on the Feelometer before practising this step: _____

C

Keep CALM:

How did you keep CALM while practising this step? _____

_____

T

THINK Strong Thoughts:

Write down the Scared Thoughts that you had: _____

_____

Write down the Strong Thoughts that you had: _____

_____

I

Get INTO Action:

When did you practise this step on your ACTION Ladder? _____

_____

My reward for climbing this step is: _____

Rating on the Feelometer after practising this step: _____

O

N

Take Action

Home Task Seven
Reviewing my ACTION Ladder

Write down the step you completed on your ACTION Ladder:

_____

THINK about how you went climbing this step on your ACTION Ladder. On the blackboard below, write down the things that went well when you practised this step.

Things that went well

THINK about the things that you could try to improve for the next step on your ACTION Ladder. On the blackboard below, write down the things that you could do differently on the next step.

Things I could improve next time

When you climb the next step on your ACTION Ladder, do the things you have written above. Remember to use all the skills in the ACTION plan as well!

Home Task Eight
Being Assertive Practice

Look for a time when you could practise being Strong, Confident and Assertive and answer the questions below.

Write down when you were Confident and Assertive (like the Strong Dolphin) on the line below:

_____

Step One: Tell the other person what you think the problem is

Step Two: Tell the other person how you feel about the problem

Step Three: Tell the other person a solution to the problem

Did you use Confident Body Signals (SMILE)? ☐ YES ☐ NO

Write down how you felt and what happened after you were Confident and Assertive on the lines below:

_____

_____

Home Task Nine
Being Assertive Practice

Answer the questions below if a time comes up when you need to use the steps for Dealing with Bullying.

Write down when you had to deal with bullying on the line below:

_____

Step One: _____

Step Two: Circle which Strong and Confident OPTIONS you chose

Walk away

Tell an adult

Ignore the bullying if you can

Say "I heard what you said and I don't really care"

Tell them firmly and calmly to leave you alone

Imagine there is a force field all around you protecting you from their words

Step Three: Did you decide on the best Option and take ACTION?

_____

Congratulate yourself for dealing with this situation!

Write down how you felt and what happened after you used the Steps for Dealing with Bullying:

_____

_____

Take Action

Notes

Take Action

Notes

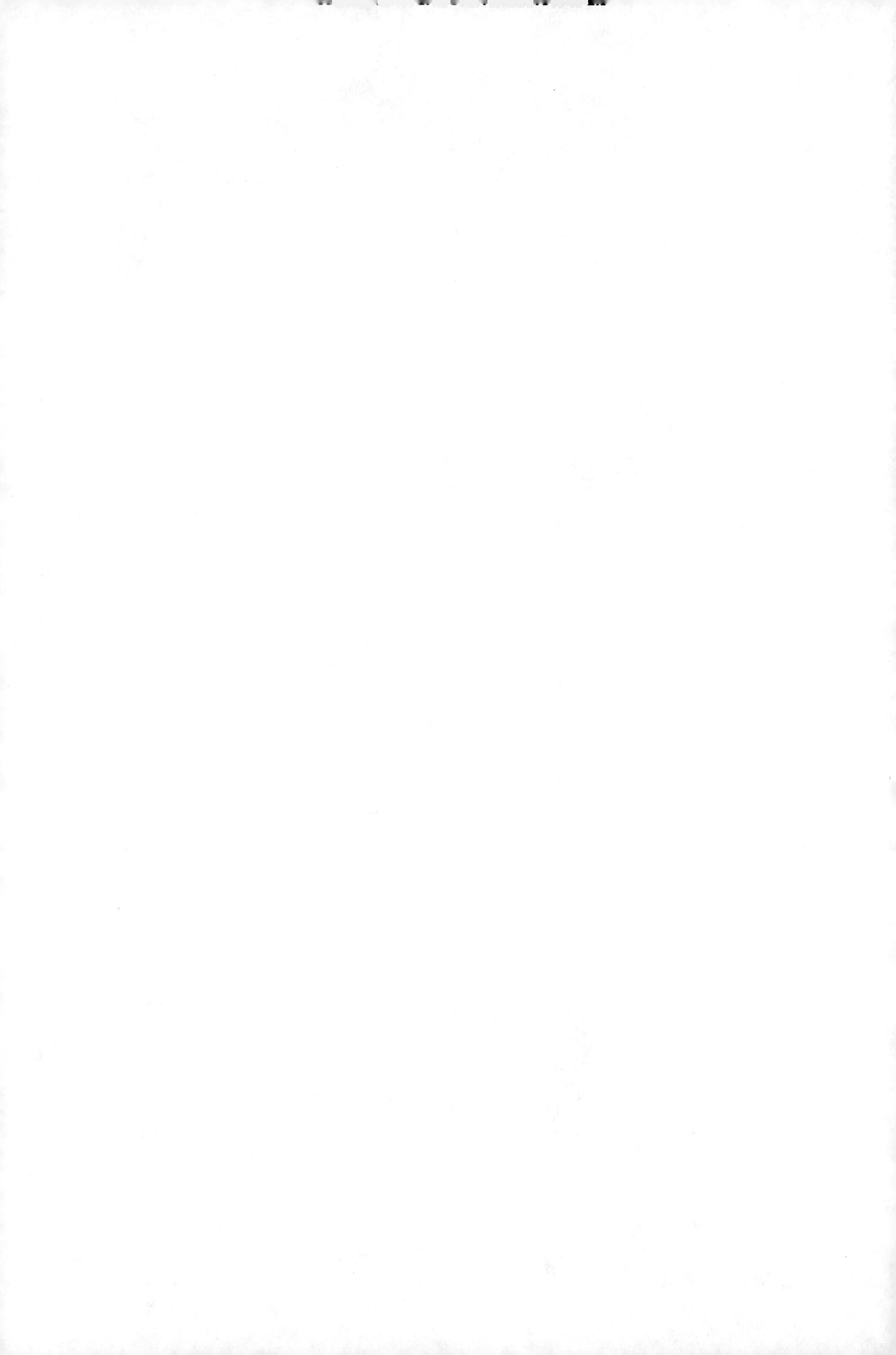

www.ingramcontent.com/pod-product-compliance
Lightning Source LLC
Chambersburg PA
CBHW081507290326
41931CB00041B/3234